YR WYDDFA
the story of Snowdon summit

YR WYDDFA

the story of Snowdon summit

Michael Senior

First published in 2010

ISBN: 978-1-84524-164-3

Cover image by kind permission of Rob Piercy
www.robpiercy.com
Images of Hafod Eryri © Ray Wood

Cover design: Eirian Evans

Published by Llygad Gwalch,
Ysgubor Plas, Llwyndyrys,
Pwllheli, Gwynedd, Wales, LL53 6NG,

www.carreg-gwalch.com

Contents

Author's Preface

At three o'clock on Saturday 14th April, 1956, I left Pen y Pass carpark, and reached the summit of Snowdon an hour and three quarters later. It was my sixteenth birthday.

On May 1st I was back; it took me the same time, but was misty that day. In all I climbed Snowdon four times that year, and three the next, one of which was an ascent by moonlight to see the dawn. I have a record of nineteen ascents during the next four decades by the Miners' Track alone, with an average speed of an hour and thirty-six minutes, the fastest of which was in 1980 at an hour and twenty-one. Over the years my climbs have been rather marred by this knowledge of competing with some twenty or so younger people, my former selves.

It was not long before I found the routes up Yr Wyddfa unacceptably populated, a characteristic which has remorselessly increased and which, I now realise, was far from new, even in the 1950's. I began to concentrate instead on the Carneddau, which I feel I have made my home territory. You can be alone there at almost any time of year, sometimes visibly alone on the whole of the upland mass; and if you do encounter someone on the summit of Carnedd Llywelyn you know a lot about them: you know, because of the process of self-selection, what sort of person they are. People do not make the effort to go so far from the beaten track for what I might regard as the wrong reason (to be able to say you have done it, for instance, or because it seems to be the right thing to do) but through some stubborn personal longing to be in a sublime and exclusive place.

Motives for reaching the summit of Yr Wyddfa have varied strikingly over the centuries, as we shall see, but during one of the times of its mass popularity, the first half of the 19th century, fashion seems to have been a spur, at least, driving everyone of note – Wordsworth, Darwin, Huxley, Ruskin, visiting royalty and fashionable elite – to make the bizarre expedition.

This book will try to convey what it meant to them, this journey into such strange surroundings, and why Snowdon's summit has held its place in our national imagination. Certainly it is impossible to be there even today, among excited schoolchildren and bedraggled dogs, waiting your turn in the queue for the summit cairn, and not to feel the thrill of being stuck out in the air on a heap of jumbled boulders with the whole world of Britain below your feet.

On the summit, 2009.

Introduction: first footsteps

King Arthur came out of Cwm Bleiddiaid over the spur of Yr Aran and saw his enemies ahead of him in Cwm Tregalan. They fled toward the ridge which divides Cwm Dyli from Cwm Llan and he descended to the valley to pursue them. It must have been about that time that he realised he had come the wrong way. There is nothing for it but to fall to the valley bottom before beginning again the trek up the eastern slope. The cliffs of Clogwyn Du are too steep to let you skirt the valley on the contour: they force you down. By the time he got up to the watershed he must have felt that there was something to be said for the thought of the level corn-fields lying either side of the river and the road running to many-tower'd Camelot.

When Arthur finally reached the ridge and saw the lake below he realised the seriousness of his mistake. The enemy had not fled, but retreated out of sight and waited. He had gone up alone, leaving his army no doubt puffing behind. Hence it was on the ridge just below Yr Wyddfa's summit that he fell to an arrow shower.

It was the second time he had been there. The giant Rhita had conquered all the kings of Britain, adding insult to injury by wearing their beards as a cloak, and issued to Arthur, the one king remaining, a challenge to part with his beard also. He said there was a gap in his cloak. Arthur declined, and the two met in single combat, on a mountain

The summit cairn and huts in the 19th century.

which is identified by the story-tellers as Snowdon, because of what happened then. Arthur slew the giant – the strongest enemy he had encountered, he said - and his knights proceeded to bury the body by heaping up over it a massive pile of stones. Each knight carried a stone up the hill, and it is thus that the summit of Snowdon came into existence. Yr Wyddfa, or more fully in its older form Gwyddfa Rhita y Gawr, the tumulus of Rhita the Giant.

It is implied by the story that it is not just the summit cairn which owes its explanation to this event, but the whole peak of the mountain itself, the pointed dome of rock. However there is no doubt that the fact that there has been for so long a cairn on this summit has led people to wonder whose burial cairn it is. According to Sir John

Rhys's informant in the 1890's "The cairn on the summit of Snowdon was the Giant's before it was demolished and made into a sort of tower which existed before the hotel was made." 'Arthur's Cairn', however, is the one which was at least until about 1850 to be seen on Bwlch y Saethau, which is, Rhys comments, not very far away. "...it would take you half an hour or perhaps a little more to walk from the one *carnedd* to the other." I would say a little less.

There is indeed a cairn as well on Bwlch y Saethau now, and it marks the point at which you can descend to Glaslyn by the scramble down y Cribau, thus combining the top of the Watkin Path with the Miners Track – but I had always assumed it was erected maybe a long time ago to mark the junction of the paths. It is too small to be a Bronze Age burial cairn, and in any case the idea that it might be the burial place of Arthur has never been seriously proposed, perhaps because the most notable thing about the once-and-future-king is that he is not dead, but transposed to the lake-isle of Avalon, awaiting there the time to return and save us, in an hour of need.

Whatever became of the king, Arthur's knights withdrew to a cave on the sheer face of Lliwedd, to rest, apparently, because when they were disturbed there by a lost shepherd many centuries later they were all asleep. *Ogof Llanciau Eryri*, the young men of Snowdonia's cave, found by the Cwm Dyli shepherd when a sheep of his had fallen onto a ledge of the cliff-face. As he squeezed into the cave and saw in the lamplit interior the amazing sight of the knights, in full armour, resting on their weapons but asleep, his head banged on a bell hanging by the entrance, and the whole lot woke up with a terrible shout. As can be imagined the shepherd, though he fled, was never quite the same again. Nor has anyone dared to repeat the adventure.

The surprisingly detailed knowledge we possess of King Arthur's movements on Yr Wyddfa do not stem from fancy but from the authority of Sir John Rhys, Professor of Celtic at Oxford University from 1877 and author of *Celtic Folklore*, published in 1901 and based on research carried out locally largely in the 1880's. On the question of Arthur's association with Snowdon Rhys was transcribing a collection of local lore published in Welsh in a magazine called *Y Brython* in 1861 under the heading of 'The History of Beddgelert Parish'. The piece in question, of September 1861, is part of a long-running series of articles at this time and, like all *Y Brython's* articles, anonymous. Sometimes the 'correspondents' who wrote them are identified on the title page, but in this case we know from other evidence that this is the work of William Jones, who was born in Beddgelert in 1829 and specialised in local folk-lore and later in geology.

It is clear that Jones was given complete credibility at the time as an authentic source of traditional material, but we have to remember that so, in the past, had been Geoffrey of Monmouth, who more or less invented British mythology, and Iolo Morganwg, the antiquarian later revealed as partly fraudulent. When Jones tells us of the route taken by Arthur from Dinas Emrys to Bwlch y Saethau we tend to believe the authenticity of the story because it is transmitted by Rhys. But there are alternatives. Either Jones was reporting genuine local lore, which may have been conveyed through generations perhaps down thousands of years; or Jones was making it

The summit itself is a mass of boulders, from early times surmounted by human constructions.

up. In either case, however, I think that in the publication of the article in *Y Brython* we have an instance of that moment at which oral lore becomes legend.

We are not told, in the story, who King Arthur's enemies were, but one of the 'Triads of Britain' specifies that a meeting of conspirators against Arthur took place in 'Nanhwynain', which is now known as Nant Gwynant, which lies below Snowdon, the purpose of which was 'to strengthen the cause of the Saxons in the Isle of Britain'. One of the conspirators was named as Medrawd, the Mordred of later story who is the ultimate destroyer of Arthur at the battle of Camlan. The personal and the political elements of the great epic have perhaps some seeds starting to germinate at this point.

* * *

Although it seems hard to believe that the summit of Snowdon is made out of stones brought up by Arthur's knights to cover the body of a dead giant, the alternative, as presented to us by modern science, is very much harder. We are invited to envisage events which took place on the shores of a giant ocean, once upon a time.

Another World

The fact is that in explaining the origins of Snowdon we have to talk of what is in effect a totally different place. There was a vast ocean, called the Iapetus. It is pronounced eye-ap-ettus, and named after the father of Atlas, in Greek mythology, and is also the name of a satellite of Saturn. This ocean was about two and a half thousand miles across at its widest, and it existed for perhaps a hundred million years about five hundred million years ago. On one side of it was what would eventually become North America, which included at this time the bit of earth which would eventually become Scotland. On the other side of it, however, was the land which would become Wales, at that time at the edge of a large continent called Gondwana, which included what is now Africa.

The idea of continental drift, on which all this information is based, was promoted by a German meteorologist called Alfred Wegener in the 1920's, specifically in a 1928 book called *The Origins of Continents and Oceans*, in which he originated the name Pangaea for the supercontinent which he deduced was the form of much of the world's land some 300 million years ago. The theory was supported by fossil distribution and mineral deposits at the time, but now Wegener's principles can be further substantiated by the science of paleomagneticism, the study of the Earth's magnetism as preserved in rocks at

The cliffs below the summit show the folded strata of which the mountain is made.

the time they were formed, which gives us data as to the latitude at which this formation took place. Rocks contain magnetic, that is iron-rich, materials, which behave like compasses, leaving, when they become fixed, a record of the Earth's magnetism at that time and place where the rock became solid.

Because of that movement of the Earth's plates on which everything on its surface rests, the relative positions of those old continents began to change, and the importance of the Iapetus Ocean to us lies in what happened when it closed. This process, which brought the shape of things nearer to one we can recognize, happened in the middle of a period known as the Ordovician, some four hundred million years ago. The two plates colliding which brought about the closing of the Iapetus threw up a chain of mountains at either shore of the former ocean. These are known as the Caledonides, and they came into existence over the course of a hundred million years, say between five hundred and four hundred million years ago. The event is known as the Caledonian Orogeny, from the Greek for mountain, *oros* and 'genesis', from the Greek for being born.

These mountains included the ranges which eventually became the Appalachians in North America, the Scandinavian mountains, the Scottish and Lake District chains, and Snowdonia. Because of the combination of faults and friction caused by the collision and buckling of the plates these mountains were volcanic, and volcanic activity went on for a considerable time and accounts for much of the surface structure of the land today.

Wales then found itself on the shores of a small continent known to geologists as Avalonia, which had split from the super-continent Gondwana. The area of the future Wales then took the form of a volcanic island emerging in a shallow sea, all resting on a continental shelf. The whole of this, to emphasise further its distance from our present standpoint, was near the equator – some fifteen to twenty degrees south. Ash flows erupted forming a surface of pumice and rhyolite, but then the volcanic crater subsided causing further ash eruption which gave a large covering of ash, some 1,700 feet thick. The sea then entered the former crater, and the whole elaborate conformation went underwater again.

This sequence, eruption, emergence, subsidence, immersion, happened several times. The variations of each, their duration and their distance ago in time involve such numbers as to dim rather than heighten our understanding. The fact is that it is the whole combination of these events which has given rise to the summit of Snowdon, and for this reason it is not possible to give a precise answer to the question 'what is it made of?', beyond the simple, if unlikely one, 'mainly volcanic ash'. To put it in summary, the formation of the Welsh Basin and then the Snowdon Volcanic Corridor went something like this: the Avalonia microcontinent moved out over what had been the Iapetus Ocean, say 446 million years ago; this and other similar movements at the time gave rise to the Caledonian Orogeny; volcanoes deposited sediments in the marine basin on the continental edge; as the microcontinent Avalonia detached from Gondwana and moved north to collide and converge with North America, in the process locking with the other half of Britain, volcanoes returned to the Welsh Basin culminating in the Snowdon Volcanic Corridor, in the late Ordovician age, say 450 million years ago. The volcanic activity caused by this activity laid down much of the rock, including the summit of Snowdon, which forms the exposed mountain tops of Snowdonia today.

Geologists call this type of rock (which I have referred to above as being made of volcanic ash), 'tuffs', which describes volcanic material welded into solid form after ejection. The other types of erupted rock have emerged from the volcanoes either in their present makeup, like granite, which had cooled below ground before being erupted, or rhyolite, which cooled at once on the surface. Snowdon is made of such matter as well, but the higher reaches are predominantly made of what was originally

Strewn boulders near the summit show that this height lay above the glacier.

fragments of the dust of heated rock.

It is often remarked, because so extraordinary and yet undeniable, that the summit of Snowdon contains the fossilized remains of marine creatures. These are embedded in the volcanic ash, and illustrate the fact that the whole thing was laid down in layers under a shallow sea.

How then did it get so hard that it is still there? We know that material formed at the relatively low pressures of the Earth's surface rather than passing from molten to solid form within the high-pressure zone of its depths, might be expected to be less dense, less closely-packed and so less durable. Here, as so often in geology, we find ourselves working backwards. Snowdon summit is still there, so it is harder than its surroundings. If a rock has survived longer than other relative examples we know that it must have undergone greater pressure, and so must have been deep in the earth when it took on its present character. Looking at the cliffs below the summit we can get a clue about how this happened. They are (seen in the right light) visibly made of curved strata, the middle lower than the ends. This form is known as a syncline, a sheet of rock in the form of a basin. If this particular part of the mountain was at the bottom of such a basin-like curve it would come under enormous pressure from its own two sides, and if all this took place deep underground the pressure would be increased.

When all this land emerged for (as far as we are concerned) the most recent time, it took the form of a giant highland dome. The next phase, which gave it its present form, was caused not by things happening within the Earth but by the effects of climate change on its surface.

In the long periods following the throwing up of the mountains, when volcanic activity caused by convergence of the plates of the Earth's crust emitted large quantities of carbon dioxide into the atmosphere, there were several instances of climate change. Global warming took place in the mezozoic period, lasting from about 245 to about 65 million years ago, the period during which the super-continent known as Pangaea broke up; and this was followed, during the Cenozoic age, by relatively sudden climate cooling. One cause of this was the previous period of mountain-building itself. The weathering of rocks now risen above the Earth's surface allowed a run-off of carbon, an accelerating process, since rain dissolves some of the CO_2 in the rocks to make a weak acid which dissolves some minerals in the rock to make a carbon-rich compound which then washes away, thus reducing the amount of carbon available to form a greenhouse gas, a main cause of global heating. The opening of the Atlantic Ocean following the separation of the parts of Pangaea caused greater doming and uplift of the rifted margins, which included Snowdonia, leading in this way to further cooling of the Earth.

As a result of tectonic activity, therefore, the climate fell into a state which was sensitive to small changes. Variations in the Earth's orbit and angle of rotation, for instance, changed the amount of solar radiation received in various parts of it, with maximum impact in the northern mid-latitudes. In the end, about two million years ago, the Earth's climate started to oscillate between glacial periods, when ice sheets covered the northern mid-latitudes, and interglacials, when there was ice only at the poles.

We tend to refer now to 'the ice age', as if there was only one, but in fact there were many. As far as we are concerned, looking at Snowdon to consider how it took its present form, only the last one counts. In the nature of things although the landscape is the result of a long succession of attacks by ice, it is only the latest one of which there is any evidence, since that removed effectively all the signs of the previous ones. Before the ice attacked it this peak, along with all others, was a part of a broad upland drained by shallow river valleys, its flanks between the valleys becoming scarred by weathering.

That form is important, because although the ice had the power to modify and aggravate, it could not build the underlying form of the land it worked on. Glaciation starts with ice forming and growing at the heads of valleys. In a stable situation it forms in the winter and melts during the summer, but something called 'positive mass balance' occurs when the accumulation of snow and ice in the winter exceeds the summer loss. This is then self-accelerating, since ice cools the air and reflects rather than absorbs the sun's heat and so itself leads to further cooling, which leads to further ice.

We can see today that this process led, at least on the last occasion, to ice sheets in these valleys a thousand feet deep. This has an interesting result, as far as the appearance of the summit of Snowdon is concerned. The whole of the lower slopes have been glacially eroded, with the result that much loose debris in the form of scattered rock has been scooped away, and the slopes smoothed and evened off: but the summit was free of the ice, being above it, and the effects can be seen quite clearly. Like its neighbours, the Glyderi and the Carneddau, Snowdon has a profusion of loose boulders near the summit which would have been carried off by a glacier if one had reached here, and the stones are weathered by erosion of frost and rain (which the lower slopes escaped) but not scraped smooth or striated by ice.

The erosion caused by the ice was rapid at first: the weathered materials from previous ages were stripped and carried off. The valley floors were gouged out by abrasion, the ice bearing rocks at its base which scratched and shovelled material it passed over. Towards the end of each ice age, and from our point of view visibly the last, the ice ate back into the mountain at its top, giving the phenomena so distinctive of this area, known as cwms. Snowdon itself is (as can readily be seen) the result of the convergence of several cwms, to be precise Cwm Dyli, Cwm Glas, Cwm Clogwyn and Cwm Tregalan. The summit is the last bit which is left after attack from all sides by erosion: and that is why it is a peak.

Early Ascents

The early references to Snowdon do not encourage going too close, let alone to the top. Giraldus Cambrensis saw it on his way to and from Anglesey, in 1188, and referred to it briefly along with the massif as a whole, as peaks which "seem to rear their lofty summits even to the clouds". William Camden, in the 16th century, took a similarly awe-struck view, telling us that the snow lay on the summits all year round. John Leland rode past in 1536, but he thought that the inner upland was "horrible with the sight of bare stones". John Speed, the map-maker, largely influenced by Camden, summed up the impressed but distant opinion, about 1610: "These mountains may not unfitly be termed the British Alpes, as being the most vaste of all Britain... all of them towering up into the aire, and round encompassing one farre higher than all the rest, peculiarly called Snowdon-Hill...." He reaffirms that they were covered in snow all the year. We get the feeling from this slight evidence that no-one actually went up Snowdon in all this time.

It is generally said that the first recorded ascent took place in 1639. In that year Thomas Johnson extended his botanical researches further than had his predecessors and contemporaries. The dedication applied by botanists at that time may well surprise us, but we have to remember that this new scientific study stemmed from a practical one which had been a busy industry for some time. It originated from herbalism, which was an important branch of medicine and in common with other residues of medieval interests, such as astronomy and chemistry, had become subjected to a new scientific rigour in the period leading to the emergence of the Enlightenment.

Johnson was born in Selby, in Yorkshire, about 1600. He became resident in London until 1626, when he moved back to northern England. Botany did not yet exist as a separate discipline, rather than a practical branch of the profession of medicine, and Johnson qualified as an apothecary in 1628. Nevertheless it was undoubtedly botany he was practising, and in fact his work laid the foundation of the study in this country. His published descriptions of expeditions to Kent and to Hampstead Heath in 1629 are said to be the earliest printed reports of such undertakings in Britain. He took up correspondence with Thomas Glynn of Glynllifon ("my very good friend"), a fellow plant collector. It was this link which led in due course to his expedition to Wales.

Johnson and two companions left London on 22nd July, and went on the old stage-coach road via Aylesbury and Stratford upon Avon, through Birmingham and Wolverhampton, to Chester. They entered Wales at Flint, and took the conventional route through Holywell and Rhuddlan to meet Thomas Glynn at Bodysgallen, where they were all guests of Robert Wynn. They crossed to Conwy, negotiated Penmaenmawr, and came via Bangor and Caernarfon to Glynllifon. It was the beginning of August by that time, and at dawn on August 3rd Johnson's party rode out to confront the British Alps, *montes totius*

Insulae maximi. The account was written up by him in Latin in *Mercurii Botanici pars altera*, in 1641.

He had a 'native boy' as guide. Snowdon was in cloud. "Leaving our horses and outer garments, we began to climb the mountain. The ascent at first is difficult, but after a bit a broad open space is found, but equally sloping, great precipices on the left, and a difficult climb on the right. Having climbed three miles, we at last gained the highest ridge of the mountain, which was shrouded in thick cloud. Here the way was very narrow, and climbers are horror-stricken by the rough rocky precipices on either hand ." When they got to such a point of the ridge that they could not proceed further, they seated themselves in the midst of the clouds, first of all to put in order the plants they had collected amongst the rocks and precipices, and then to eat the food they had brought up with them.

In other words, it is by no means certain that on this, the first recorded ascent, the walkers actually reached the summit. They did not actually know how far they had got, because they were enclosed in mist. They did not, at any rate, describe anything like the summit peak, which would be identified in any conditions. Another thing is rather more positively notable about this account. It was clearly not by any means the first time visitors had been up the peak, or the guide would not have told them that climbers are horror-stricken by the cliffs on either side of the path (which they could not see, because of the shrouding mist). Moreover the availability of a guide itself tells us much: people had been here before, and as a matter of course, since the business was organized. And of course the guide himself had been to the summit of the mountain, for whatever reasons, more than once.

After Johnson, and particularly after the publication of the Mercurii, others were inspired to make the trip, during the 17th century. A botanist named John Ray made two expeditions, in 1658 and 1662, the second of which was recorded in his 'Third Itinerary'. Ray was perhaps the first botanist whose interest in plants was not based on their medicinal properties, but he was said to have studied plants merely so that he could learn more about them. In fact during the years that spanned the lifetimes of Thomas Johnson and John Ray (Dewi Jones points out, in his meticulously researched book *The Botanists and Mountain Guides of Snowdonia*) botany began to emerge as a subject in its own right. On one of the occasions when Ray came the summit was in clouds, but he found plants which were new to him. "Incidentally," remarks Dewi Jones, "on his return journey home through Bala and Shrewsbury Ray heard about the death of Oliver Cromwell."

Ray was in correspondence with Edward Lhuyd, (who became perhaps the most notable of the botanists to bring Snowdon into prominence during the 17th century) though Dewi Jones says that it is not known if they ever met. Lhuyd is chiefly eminent as the discoverer of the Snowdon lily, which Ray then listed in the second edition of his Synopsis, of 1696, as *Bulbosa Alpina juncifolia, pericarpio unico erecto in summo cauliculo dodrantali*, according to the clearly unwieldy system then used, which Linnaeus tidied up with his new notation to *Anthericum serotinum*, and which today is known after its discoverer as *Lloydia serotina*.

Lhuyd found forty new plants in Snowdonia that

The Snowdon Lily is a tiny plant easily overlooked when not in flower.

summer, of 1688. Among other revelations he corrected the previously current view as to Snowdon's snows, saying that "Generally speaking, there's no snow here from the end of April to the midst of September", which is roughly the case at present. His interest in Wales was more than botanical – he was born near Oswestry – and his notes about the places and population of Wales were used in the 1695 revised edition of Camden's *Britannia*.

The Snowdon lily is a very small white flower (no more than four inches tall) which is also to be found on the Glyders, but is otherwise exclusively alpine. It flowers in June, and when not in flower cannot be easily distinguished, since its leaves, though quite long, are as thin as grass. It now cannot be found in accessible places, so that in effect its extinction has been halted by its rarity.

Lhuyd, who became Keeper of Kew Gardens, spent much of his later career studying fossils. One of his assistants, John Lloyd of Corwen, took up his work on Snowdon's plants, using the same local guide to take him from Nant Peris to their habitats. He it is who gives us our first glimpse of what the summit was like before it became a tourist destination. In the summer of 1686:

> There is a wall rais'd on ye top of ye Hill, made like a sheep fold, where we shelter'd for a while, & carved our names in stones as several others had done before us, for we were as willing to be famouse as they.

That tells us for certain that the habit of walking to the summit existed before 1686. It also points to a characteristic of people succeeding in this personally significant achievement: the need to tell someone about it, a requirement made harder before the time of the summit huts and now dealt with effectively by the mobile phone – "Guess where I am!" being perhaps the most frequently uttered exclamation there today. R. H. Newell, a writer whom we shall be meeting again shortly, commented, in 1821, at the very threshold of organised and better recorded trips:

> It is amusing to observe the anxiety of the adventurers to record their exploit: scraps of paper are carefully packed among stones at the top, with their names, and the date of their excursion.

Clogwyn Du'r Arddu was a challenge to the botanist before the rock-climber.

Although this evidence points to a new attitude becoming evident at the end of the 17th century, the purpose of the botanists who pioneered the ascents remained rigidly functional. They were supplying the museums, horticultural institutions and private collections which were now a formal infrastructure of the new science. They did not come to refresh their souls in the mountain air. They came to collect a root of thrift or mountain sorrel, campion, sandwort, arctic saxifrage or Alpine saw-wort, to be the first to catalogue *arabis petraea*, the northern rock-cress at one time common at Clogwyn Du'r Arddu, to furnish the Westminster Physic Garden or Edward Morgan's Medical Garden with a world-leading collection. The Arctic-alpines which flourished then on the lime-rich cliffs just below the summit were rare enough to make a reputation in the small world of pioneering botanists.

The existence of the wall at the top however tells us that something else was happening at this time: somebody had built it, evidently, to provide shelter for the travellers who reached there. Perhaps the moment of transition from science to recreation is identifiable in the various ascents made by the Reverend William Bingley. Bingley came as an undergraduate in 1798 and again in 1801, on the first occasion pursuing at least a nominal programme of seeking rare plants. He came to Snowdon first from Caernarfon and was unimpressed by the easy ascent from the Llanberis side – "the ascent is so gradual , that a person, mounted on a little Welsh poney, may ride up very nearly to the top." He deviated from the track to investigate Clogwyn Du'r Arddu, "to search that rock for some plants which Lhwyd and Ray have described as growing there", and in the process undertook the first recorded rock climb. After the hazardous climb of the Clogwyn he and his companion were so exhilarated by reaching the ridge that they pounded up the rest of the peak: "after the labour of climbing the steep of Clogwyn Du'r Arddu" he "found ascending to the summit of Snowdon perfectly easy."

It is, he tells us, 1190 yards "(somewhat less than a quarter of a mile)" from sea level. "It rises to a mere point, its summit not being more than three or four yards in diameter." He was impressed by the view: on a clear day (which evidently this was) he says one can see the hills of Scotland, the mountains of Yorkshire, Westmoreland and Cumberland, and some hills in Lancashire; Ireland in the other direction, and the isle of Man. The whole of

Caernarfonshire and Meirionnydd in between. He comments that this is a rare experience: it is so often shrouded in mist that "except when the weather is perfectly fine and settled, the traveller through this country will find it somewhat difficult to have a day sufficiently clear to permit him to ascend the mountain with any degree of pleasure." Bingley reports that there is a spring of fresh water near the summit, a fact not however mentioned by others, which he evidently experienced since he said it was the coldest he could remember tasting. Bingley thinks the ascent is easily within the ability of "a person in good health and spirits". He recommends an early start, "to be upon the journey by five or six o'clock in the morning", and the employment of a guide, "for otherwise a sudden change in the weather might render the attempt extremely perilous to a stranger".

Bingley was so much attracted by the experience of reaching the top that he went again twice during the next few days, from the Llyn Cwellyn side. On his second return, on a perfect cloudless day, the guide suddenly told them while they were picnicking on the summit that a storm was coming. They packed up the picnic and hurried off the summit but were caught by a downpour and thick mist a short way down. Battered by hailstones and with water over their boots they tried to shelter, in a blanked out world. Half an hour later the sun was shining again and the wet world sparkling.

Bingley had decided to take all the paths up Snowdon then in existence, and he finally went with a small party of people up from Beddgelert. He makes much of the narrow crossing of Clawdd Coch, which evidently had a reputation by then for frightening climbers: "Many instances have occurred of persons who, having passed over it in the night, were so terrified at seeing it by day-light the next morning, that they have not dared to return the same way, but have taken a very circuitous route by Bettws." Evidently by the end of the 18th century the habit of going up by night to see the sunrise was already well established.

Bingley was conscious that in writing about northern Wales he was following in the footsteps of Thomas Pennant, who dates his 'Tour in North Wales' at 1773. Pennant came up what is now the Snowdon Ranger path, over the cliffs of Bwlch Cwm Brwynog and above the du'r Arddu valley. The summit, he says, is called Yr Wyddfa meaning *The Conspicuous*, which his editor (John Rhys) says is a "very pretty" interpretation, but "the meaning is more probably to be sought in the word *gwydd*, wood, which would connect the name with the mountain as a Royal Forest." The summit, Pennant says, "rises almost to a point, or, at best, there is but room for a circular wall of loose stones, within which travellers usually take their repast."

He accurately describes the structure of the peak: "propped by four vast buttresses" with cwms between them. He describes the view, of Cheshire, Yorkshire, Scotland and Ireland, the Isle of Man, Anglesey. On a previous occasion, he remembers, he had come up by night, and he gives us perhaps our first description of the famous dawn: the gradual revelation of the land and the sea as the light unrolled across it. This time, however, the one he is mainly describing, he was not so lucky with the weather. He describes the familiar swirling of mist and its dramatic breaks onto open distant views. On the way down they were overtaken by a thunderstorm, experiencing, and summarizing for us, Snowdon's monumental weather.

> It is very seldom that the traveller gets a proper day to ascend *Snowdon*; for often, when it appears clear, it becomes suddenly and unexpectedly enveloped in mist, by its attraction of clouds, which just before seemed remote and at great heights.

Pennant gives various measurements for the height of Snowdon – twelve hundred and forty yards, as measured by a Mr. Caswell in 1682, or more recently one thousand one hundred and eighty nine yards and one foot, "from the quay at Caernarvon to the highest peak." He deals very briefly with its geology ("Large coarse crystals are often found in the fissures") and its wild-life, which includes the "antient inhabitant" the goat, becoming daily less in value "since the decline of orthodox wigs, to which its snowy hair universally contributed."

Snowdon was, at the time, a royal forest. This is to do with the rights to take game, and the area known for this purpose as Snowdon actually stetched as far as Meironydd and Anglesey, "with the view," Pennant says, "of gratifying the rapacity of the favorite *Dudley*, earl of *Leicester*, who had been appointed chief ranger." The deer which formed the principal asset of this 'forest' were killed off on Snowdon itself during the early 17th century; but the title of 'Ranger' which went with the designation lingered around the mountain, until finally giving the name to the Snowdon Ranger path. This is claimed in the pages of Borrow's *Wild Wales* to have been instigated by the most prominent mountain guide of the time, who called himself the Snowdon Ranger and his house the same, a name it still bears now as a youth hostel and bore formerly as an inn. "A ranger means a guide, sir," his son-in-law tells Borrow, innocent of any knowledge of the royal forest and the earl of Leicester, "my father-in-law is generally termed the Snowdon Ranger because he is a tip-top guide..."

Pennant provides a clue as to the possible origin of the habit by then become popular of spending the night on the summit, with the aim of seeing the dawn: "It is still said, what whosoever slept upon *Snowdon*, would wake inspired, as much as if he had taken a nap on the hill of *Apollo*." Among much other information he gives us, while on the subject of the mountain, is that the title Lord of Snowdon was that which Llywelyn was most reluctant to yield to Edward I (though in Llywelyn's case, as often, 'Snowdon' stands for the inner heartland which we might today call Snowdonia). He says that one of Edward's first acts on winning the war was to hold a 'triumphal fair' on the mountain, before the more elaborate tournaments which he held at Nefyn. He dismisses, like other writers, the commonly held notion that the mountain is snow-covered all year: "there being frequently whole weeks, even in winter, in which they are totally free."

Though at this period the only concession to tourism seems to have been the building of a semi-circular stone wall, like a sheep pen, around the summit, we can see the increasing habit which climbers had of taking their picnics there and even spending the night in the wall's shelter, leading inevitably to the construction of the huts. The wall itself is said to have formed the boundary between the two great estates which rose to this point: that of Faenol, which covered the area of the later quarries around Llanberis, and the Bulkeley estate based at Baron Hill in Anglesey, which included much of the southern stretches of the mountain.

Perhaps the last person to write about this older version of the summit was R. H. Newell, whose book was published in 1821 but seems to recall experiences of a few years earlier. It takes the form of a series of letters to his son, who is proposing to undertake a sketching tour of northern Wales. He shows the influence of both Pennant and Bingley in his background information, but some of the practical advice is personal.

Newell was, it seems, conscious of his position at the end of a period of style which has become known as the picturesque. He went along with the principles of it, to the extent that he accepted the assumption that one travels in order to sketch, and that there are certain rules for seeing the landscape around one which relate to the way it will look on paper. He said that "Picturesque is, indeed, a word which now almost palls upon the ear", but that to him it still meant "that peculiar kind of beauty which is agreeable in a picture". Snowdon itself had not been a subject considered suitable for the type of work then considered acceptable. Newell says that he has never seen a drawing done from, rather than of, Snowdon, except for one done from the peak, looking towards the sea, in a water colour exhibition of 1817. Cader Idris, he says, is more picturesque. It is true that the great landscape artists viewed Snowdon from a distance - Richard Wilson, for

Richard Wilson's view of Snowdon is from the Nantlle direction.

instance, in the 1770's, from the unusual direction of Rhyd Ddu and Dyffryn Nantlle.

Newell saw Wales, as late as about 1820, as being a foreign country: "its features, inhabitants, language, manners and customs, are so very different from those of England..." His view of it is to some extent coloured by a reading of the antiquarians; he repeats Camden's description of Snowdonia as 'the British Alps'. He reasserts that it is not true about the year-long snow: "there is seldom any between the months of June and November." His experience of the summit however is factual and first-hand. "The temperature at the top is generally very low, even in the midst of summer. In July, just after sun-rise, the thermometer has been observed at 34 degrees, and in August at 46, early in the afternoon." For this reason he is explicit about what to wear.

> Let this then be your dress. Jacket, waistcoat, trowsers, and gaiters of the stuff called Jean – light and strong... top the whole with a straw, or rather willow hat. Nor must an umbrella by any means be forgotten, it is a trusty useful servant, choose it of silk, and of the largest size.

On his own ascent Newell experiences the vagaries of weather which so often impressed the travellers. On his way up from Beddgelert "suddenly a cloud came rolling past, and poured heavy rain upon us, while the whole prospect beneath was glowing with sunshine." He repeats the assertion corrected in Pennant by his editor, that Yr Wyddfa means 'The Conspicuous'. He is a little disparaging about the view from the stop, saying that though the prospect is vast, "surely its character may be understood from an inferior elevation; and what is gained by *fancying* you see a speck, which the guide *tells* you is the Isle of Man?" He prefers the close-up views of the make-up of the mountain which are to be enjoyed on the way up: "the caverns, lakes, precipices, and other peculiar features, are exceedingly grand and curious."

> The air is sharp on the top of Snowdon, but you may bear it without the help of *brandy*. There really needs no previous preparation whatever. The walk is rather laborious, but may be leisurely taken in five

hours, and the whole distance is about ten miles. It is amusing to observe the anxiety of the adventurers to record their exploit: scraps of paper are carefully packed among the stones at the top, with their names, and the date of their excursion.

The Settlement of the Summit

It was, according to D. E. Jenkins's 1899 book *Bedd Gelert*, a copper miner from Amlwch named Morris Williams, who first had the idea of providing refreshments on the summit, in 1837 or 8. Williams had observed, while working in the mines on Snowdon, how many people climbed it during the summer, and to begin with, according to Jenkins, he tried providing refreshments for them without a hut – tea, coffee, butter, bread and cheese – which convinced him that this could become a worthwhile job. The first hut was built just below the summit cairn, on land belonging to Hafod y Llan farm. It was made of stone on the outside, and lined with planed planks. Morris Williams had the disadvantage that he could not speak or understand English, and recognizing this as a drawback he took into partnership one of the guides, also called Williams, and added a touch of theatre to the whole thing by dressing in a goat-skin suit to make himself look like a savage. The hut and associated business paid off.

Jenkins is on the whole reliable, working from local informants, but Robert Jones in *The complete guide to Snowdon* says that a hut of sorts preceded that of Williams, a round shelter made out of the stones of the old wall, which could be used by climbers spending the night there from 1815. Carr and Lister, however, in *The Mountains of Snowdonia*, say that this hut was built from the dismantled

In the 19th century the summit was often reached on horseback.

wall about 1820, "some ten yards below the summit". Both
sources say the cairn itself was the next structure to be built
there, in 1827, a pile of stones set up by the Royal Engineers
undertaking a national survey. It was replaced in 1841 by a
much larger one, which appears in the early sketches and
oldest photographs, and a tall pole was added to this.

Jenkins tells how the competition soon started,
following the success of the Williams' venture. A guide
called John Roberts gained the approval of one of the
owners of the peak, Bulkeley of Baron Hill, and built a
structure on the Llanberis side. The original instigator,
Morris Williams, sold his share of the first hut to his
brother Philip, who further simplified the business by going
into partnership with his rival, John Roberts. The
partnership broke up, however, when Roberts gained a

The proximity to Snowdon added to the fashionable popularity of victorian Llanberis.

licence to sell alcohol and refused to share it with Philip Williams. It turned out that the summit was in two separate parishes, Beddgelert and Caernarfon, and in due course Williams succeeded in gaining a separate licence. "And from that day to this," writes Jenkins, "two licenses are granted for the summit, one at Carnarvon and one at Portmadoc."

It was then that the tradition began of two rival huts operating at the summit, that of John Roberts who ran it for the Royal Victoria Hotel in Llanberis, and that of the Dolbadarn Hotel, confusingly run by another Roberts, William. By 1850, when a Mr. H. Humphreys published his *Guide to the Summit of Snowdon*, the settlement then known to the guides as 'the little town of Snowdonia' consisted of four wooden huts and a gathering of guides

The expeditions to the summit became fashionable in the late 19th century.

and sellers of plant species. One of the huts was called Saxony, "because the King of Saxony dined in it – or sat in it, or possibly dosed in it, - perhaps all three." We are aware of the fashionableness of the climb, at this time. "Supper, a bed, and breakfast, are procurable there for five shillings; and during the summer seasons vast numbers of tourists avail themselves of the wretched accommodation afforded there, for the sake of seeing the sun set and rise – a truly glorious sight!" Improvements were taking place, in this busy place.

> Those huts are to be immediately papered, and to be provided with good fires, and they say, good beds too, and, strange enough, views – guide-books – stationery, &c., are to be brought there... What a change from the majesty of scenery where we had

William Williams – a Snowdon Guide.

been standing a short time before! We step from the sublime (if not to the ridiculous) to a vulgar, and very dingy hut, about 12 feet long and 9 feet wide, a rusty stove in one corner and a black coffee-pot keeping

Ruins of stables still lie below the summit on the Llanberis side.

itself warm upon it! The wooden floor damp and wet as that of a vault, the paper black and falling off, the windows abut 18 inches square, frames inclusive.

I quote from the lengthy extract from Humphreys's book given in Dewi Jones's, which gives us a clear insight into the enthusiastic commercialization of the summit and to its rather squalid condition, at the middle of the 19th century. This was how the many distinguished visitors experienced it – T. H. Huxley, for instance, who came up from Pen y Pass in 1860. This state of affairs lasted until it was decided by the various landowners to transfer the rights to the summit to the 'Tramway Company', but even then they could not ignore the demands of the public, and (according to Jenkins) the Tramway Company handed over the whole business to Miss Amos, who "opens out at Easter, and closes for the winter about the last week in September". Miss Amos kept records, evidently, and when Jenkins writes, in the 1890's, "An average of about one hundred and fifty per day visit the summit from April to June, and of no less than seven hundred from July to the second week in September." Between fifteen and twenty people can be given beds to spend the night to see the sunrise.

Fortunately we have plenty of direct testimony available to us as to what exactly it was like in the days before the train. The hut run by one of the Roberts's on behalf of the Victoria Hotel, Llanberis, kept a Visitors Book, during the mid-19th century, in which many of the climbers recorded their impressions. Most of the entries are hard to read, close-writ in slanting hand often with much fashionable flourish, but among those legible a constant complaint about the weather becomes a running theme. "Come up Snowdon, but could not see anything", writes a Mr. Drew of Surrey, in July 1847. A visitor from London echoes: "the weather was so thick that [we] could not see 10 yards down the mountain." "Made the ascent from Llanberis in 2 ¾ hours .... Through a miserable drizzling rain – saw little or nothing but a fine specimen of mountain mist – " They often mention that they came up on ponies, with a guide ("accompanied by Richard Owen – an excellent guide"). Every part of the country is featured – Cheltenham, Liverpool, Nottingham – and several Oxford and Cambridge colleges specified. There is even one entry in Latin – and one in Welsh. The books' entrants are much given to verse, the challenge of finding rhymes for 'Snowdon' being enthusiastically taken up: blow'd on, rode on, strode on – and just occasionally the weather cleared, and from the normal lament of "all mist, mist" or "Clouds, clouds, clouds. Splendid view, could see about ten yards before us", we are plunged into the problem of finding words for a totally new experience.

> After partaking of supper we went out at 10 oclock, and the scene that presented itself surpassed in grandeur anything we ever before witnessed..."

or

> ...was amply rewarded for the toil incurred in the ascent by one of the most splendid prospects I ever witnessed...

in terms which reveal the struggle to express the ineffable.

One feature of interest in these most primary of primary sources is the habit the writers had of doing little sketches, signalling, as so often in diaries and letters of the time, the need for the camera, not to say of Facebook. As a result we can see what they looked like, and even more interestingly how they saw themselves. The men often wore full-scale top hats, the women voluminous skirts. Sometimes the men had low round hats, or even caps. The women wore a bonnet and a shawl, and carried a small frilly umbrella, which evidently proved useless, being in at least one case blown inside out. The men's coats were buttoned all the way down the front, and they carried their

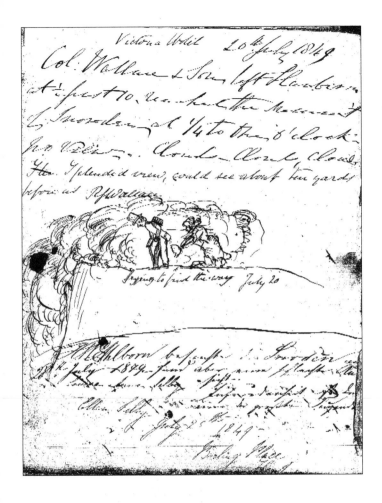

A page from the Visitors Book at the summit 'hotel'
reveal visitors' views of themselves in the 1840's and 50's.

In the summit Visitors Book, travellers added sketches of themselves.

provisions in a little box strapped to their backs. The men all smoked pipes, and in one case a woman too, if we are to believe the self-view of Mr. and Mrs Howard, on July 27th 1848, "viewed on the top of Snowdon." There is one sketch apparently joking about this habit called "View from the top of Snowdon in a mist" which shows a pipe-smoker leaning against the hut with another sitting nearby, and a figure probably representing the mountain itself smoking a pipe in the background. One of the most interesting drawings, although the pencilling appears to have faded, is of the "Interior of the Summit Hotel, Snowdon", which show very limited accommodation, but with a kitchen and a large round table.

It is clear that the purpose of all this is to see the dawn. This is admittedly self-selecting evidence, since the entries

The summit cairn sketched in the Visitors Book, dated August 4th, 1849.

in the Visitors Books are the work of people stuck, often sleepless, in the primitive hut all night. The reward is partly the feeling of good fortune, since success is far from guaranteed. Jenkins says a friend of his had been up over thirty times before he had a clear day, but "testifies that three times thirty ascents would have been amply rewarded by one sunrise." He cites a famous occasion in 1862 when

A sketch in the Visitors Book showing the inside of the 'Snowdon Hotel'.

a group of twelve went up after the Carnarvon Eisteddfod, and found the refreshment booth already crowded. He quotes the eyewitness account in *Golud yr Oes*:

> See, a brightness like an angel's smile lightens the fringe of the east; again, a bolder and more animated flash, of a crescent form, thrills the sky into a blush, and vaster riches bubble forth from an eternal store,

until the woolly clouds are borderd round with amber gilding; wave upon wave of splendour break in golden form upon the horizon....

The two whole pages of this enthusiasm as quoted by Jenkins amply illustrate the point which the writer makes halfway through: that you cannot do it in words. Indeed he was struck by the 'tangible silence' which fell on the waiting crowd: "Man's highest eloquence is muteness, and nothing else becomes a deep emotion."

The Romantics

By the time this habit of staying on Snowdon summit overnight had become something of a tradition - an expression of a vigorous, adventurous, hearty form of mid-Victorian enthusiasm – a revolution in European artistic and literary fashion had been taking place. It is often said that Wordsworth's long poem *The Prelude* was the supreme example of the Romantic attitude in England. He set the 'Conclusion' of the monumental work on the summit of Snowdon. Romanticism was essentially a reaction to the way of thought which became known as the Enlightenment, and it sought to restore a balance between Man and Nature by promoting the spirit of imagination and awe in the face of the primal powers of wild landscape. Its thinking followed the late 18th century preoccupation with the 'Picturesque' (the mood of Wordsworth's early poems) and went with the consciousness of the 'sublime', meaning awe-inspiring, as seen in the violence and grandeur of the natural world, particularly in its large-scale manifestations.

It was to see the sunrise that William Wordsworth set out from Beddgelert with his friend Robert Jones, in the summer of 1793. Jones, who lived at Plas y Llan in Denbighshire, had been a contemporary of his at Cambridge. He is referred to as 'a fellow student' in an earlier passage in *The Prelude*, and because of his keenness

William Wordsworth

as a mountaineer became a walking-companion to the budding poet when the two left university. Wordsworth visited him in Wales in the summer of 1791, and the two went to France together in 1792. Jones later took holy orders and became a curate in Wales, and later had a living in Oxfordshire, but maintained his Welsh connections. By 1793 when they came to Snowdon, William, then aged twenty-three, had published a few poems, at a time before his collaboration with Coleridge led to their first notable success (with the *Lyrical Ballads* in 1798) and before his crucial move to live in Grasmere in 1799.

The Prelude is explicitly an autobiographical poem – sub-titled "Growth of a Poet's Mind" – dealing with his memories of youthful expeditions, written over a period of years between 1799 and 1805, concerned with his formative years of the earlier 1790's. Ernest de Selincourt, in the critical edition, considers that "the account of the ascent of Snowdon was written at some earlier date", since it is carefully copied into the relevant notebook by an assistant. Wordsworth said that poetry took its form from "emotion recollected in tranquility", so that this treatment of his memory of Snowdon fulfills his ideals.

> In one of those excursions (may they ne'er
> Fade from remembrance!) through the Northern tracts
> Of Cambria ranging with a youthful friend,
> I left Bethgelert's huts at couching-time,
> And westward took my way, to see the sun
> Rise, from the top of Snowdon. To the door
> Of a rude cottage at the mountain's base
> We came, and roused the shepherd who attends
> The adventurous stranger's step, a trusty guide;
> Then, cheered by short refreshment, sallied forth.

In careful detail the climb in mist and the decline from casual conversation to solitary thoughts are described with plain realism. Nothing broke the monotony of the enclosing damp mist, until the small incident of the shepherd's dog finding a hedgehog took on the aspect of an important event - "for even such it seemed /In that wild place and at the dead of night" - until, once over, it evaporated, and "on we wound/In silence as before." An hour went by. Wordsworth happened to be ahead of the other two, when something miraculous happened: they broke clear of the cloud.

Those to whom this has happened will not forget the shock of looking out over the top of the white, endless sea of shining cloud, with sharp black peaks breaking it like rocks in a foam. It takes all Wordsworth's power of description to master the emotion the recollection of which even now takes my breath away.

> ...at my feet
> Rested a silent sea of hoary mist.
> A hundred hills their dusky backs upheaved
> All over this still ocean; and beyond,
> Far, far beyond, the solid vapours stretched,
> In headland, tongues and promontory shapes,
> Into the main Atlantic, that appeared
> To dwindle, and give up his majesty,
> Usurped upon as far as the sight could reach.

Consistent with the programme of Romanticism, this experience on Snowdon is of interest to Wordsworth for the message it bears about the human place in this order: the spiritual correspondence between the small, lost people on the mountain and the vast expanse of the natural world. The poem then becomes concerned with this transcendence, and one realizes what function the

George Borrow

adventure of climbing the mountain at night has served.

When into air had partially dissolved
That vision, given to spirits of the night
And three chance human wanderers, in calm thought
Reflected, it appeared to me the type
Of a majestic intellect, its acts
And its possession, what it has and craves,

What in itself it is, and would become.
There I beheld the emblem of a mind
That feeds upon infinity, that broods
Over the dark abyss, intent to hear
Its voice issuing forth to silent light
In one continuous stream; a mind sustained
By recognitions of transcendent power,
In sense conducting to ideal form,
In soul of more than mortal privilege.

The poem does not return to literal description of the surroundings, but continues with meditation on the individual's place in the world, and only becomes explicit again on the subject of his friends, his sister Dorothy, and Coleridge, to whom it is addressed.

Wordsworth led the way in English literature into the Romantic age, and there followed much attention to the position of the individual hero, cast, by rebellion or aesthetic obsession, into the natural world beyond urban and normal social conventions. One person who lived in this style some of his normal life as well as in his literature was George Borrow, who started travelling widely in Europe in his twenties, studying languages and customs. He made a special study of European and British gypsies. He wrote a series of books based on these experiences, *Wild Wales*, published in 1862, being the last of those semi-autobiographical accounts.

In Wales Borrow took the new turnpike roads, always travelling on foot, striding eventually along the mountain roads around Capel Curig. "Perhaps in the whole world there is no region more picturesquely beautiful than

Snowdon, a region of mountains, lakes, cataracts, and groves, in which Nature shows herself in her most grand and beautiful forms." He called Snowdon "one of the very celebrated hills of the world".

Borrow climbed Snowdon from Llanberis with "a young lad" as a guide, and his daughter Henrietta for company, Mrs. Borrow staying behind in the village, considering herself not up to it. Borrow, in characteristic ebullient form, set off singing, in Welsh. It is interesting to find that the Llanberis path was already, by then, crowded.

> We were far from being the only visitors to the hill this day; groups of people, or single individuals, might be seen going up or descending the path as far as the eye could reach. The path was remarkably good, and for some way the ascent was anything but steep.

"Feeling now rather out of breath" they sat and rested above cwm du'r Arddu, before undertaking "the real difficulty of the ascent". Henrietta persevered, as the path grew steeper, and at last they stood, panting, "upon the very top of Snowdon, the far-famed Wyddfa."

It was 1854, catering already in operation on the summit, and Borrow takes time, before releasing his emotions, to describe the scene.

> The Wyddfa is about thirty feet in diameter and is surrounded on three sides by a low wall. In the middle of it is a rude cabin, in which refreshments are sold, and in which a person resides throughout

the year, though there are few or no visitors to the hill's top, except during the months of summer.

He describes the view – "a scene inexpressibly grand" – consisting of most of Wales, part of Cumberland, the Irish Sea, and "what might be either a misty creation or the shadowy outline of the hills of Ireland." He then lectures his daughter on the importance of where they are, quoting poetry in Welsh, much to the amusement of three or four English people, and to the interest of a Welsh gentleman, who approached him. He asked if he came from Brittany, to which Borrow replied that he wished he did, evidently stung by the mockery of the English bystanders. He wished he was anything but what he was, "'one of a nation amongst whom any knowledge save what relates to money-making and over-reaching is looked upon as a disgrace. I am ashamed to say that I am an Englishman.'" It was not, of course, exactly a fashionable thing to say, and illustrates, as so often in *Wild Wales*, the author's defiant, near-pugnacious, sense of confidence in his own opinions.

Four hours after setting off they returned to the anxious Mrs. Borrow in Llanberis.

Theodore Watts-Dunton, some thirty years younger than Borrow, had known the great adventurer when he, Watts-Dunton, was in his late thirties, and probably through him gained an obsession with gypsies which inspired much of his verse and his main work of prose. He wrote the introductions to Borrow's *Lavengro* and *The Romany Rye*, which he edited, and he became a great advocate for the Romantic movement. Wilfred Noyce, in his admirable chapter ('The Writer in Snowdonia') in

Snowdon Biography, calls Watts-Dunton's book *Aylwin* the novel "which most places Snowdon among its characters".

By the time *Aylwin* was published, in 1898, the railway ran to the top of Snowdon, but you would not think this likely from the depiction of the mountain in the book: a primal backdrop of mists and chasms against which the novel's characters play out their drama. Briefly, the hero, Henry Aylwin, spends the book searching for his beloved, who has been driven to madness by a curse which fell on her as a result of a jewelled cross stolen by her father from his father's corpse. Although Watts-Dunton was a solicitor by occupation and lived in London, the book shows a surprisingly detailed knowledge of Snowdon itself, and the inns and villages of the area at the time. The search for the heroine is rather random as well as lengthy and obsessive, and it mainly provides opportunities to express Watts-Dunton's fascination for the way of life of the gypsies, seen as true natives of the world of the Romantics, a way of life which expressed the idea of a people in tune with the natural world, rather as the early travellers saw that of the American Indians. They understood the spirit of a place, indeed of Snowdon: "the mysterious magic of yr Wyddfa, that magic which no other mountain in Europe exercises". The mood of the book is suited to the idea of the supernatural qualities of Snowdon: "Then I felt coming over me strange influences which afterwards became familiar to me – influences which I can only call the spells of Snowdon." Glaslyn, known in the book as the Knockers' Llyn, had a powerful fascination for the author, as does the famous Snowdon sunrise: "Along the rough path we went,

Theodore Watts-Dunton

while the morning gradually broke over the east. Great isles and continents of clouds were rolled and swirled from peak to peak, from crag to crag, across steaming valley and valley..."

As with Borrow, we are aware that the summit itself is by now becoming part of a public domain. On top, they took "some bread and cheese and ale in the cabin there." Going back down they heard "the musical chant of a Welsh guide ahead of us, who was conducting a party of happy tourists to Llanberis." On another occasion:

> Reaching the top, we sat down in the hut and made our simple luncheon. Winnie [the heroine] was a great favourite with the people there, and she could not get away from them for a long time.

It is noticeable that in the descriptions of both George Borrow and Watts-Dunton there appears to be only one hut at the summit, whereas Humphreys, in 1850, describes a small settlement. Watts-Dunton wrote the book over a considerable period, and he may well have been remembering an early visit. The most likely explanation is that even when there were several huts they were seen as accumulations around one main one, presumably the 'Snowdon Hotel' run by Roberts for the Victoria.

The world of the Romantics (among whom Watts-Dunton would have wished to be included) was itself based on nostalgia, like the subject-matter of the pre-Raphaelite painters who also feature in *Aylwin*: a harking back to what was seen as having been better times, from a world which was by then recognizably changing. Snowdon was seen by some of the visitors as a symbol of defiance in the face of this change. But already it was necessary to seek out its wilder places. Going up the Glaslyn side, the gypsy girl says to Aylwin: "You know this is the only way to see the hills. You may ride up the Llanberis side in a go-cart."

The Huts to the Railway

"One dare not imagine," writes the editor of the 1932 Golden Treasury edition of *The Prelude*, "what Wordsworth's feelings would be in these days at the sight of the huts and a railway station on Snowdon summit!" But even by Wordsworth's time a sort of high-road to the summit existed, and in the course of the next generation to his the attitude to the achievement of reaching it had changed: it was a communal, public activity, not one for the solitary soul. The gypsy girl said to Henry Aylwin, in the novel, that you can go up from Llanberis in a go-cart, which might not have been strictly true: the path was good, but not suitable for wheeled vehicles. The first ascent with a horse and cart is said to be in 1869, carrying a barrel of pitch to fuel the beacon to be lit there to celebrate the coming of age of the heir of the Vaynol estate. In 1836 Thomas Roscoe reported one guide as complaining to another that "ponies and the easy-chairs" are "all the fashion now!" The guides were used by then to carrying heavy parcels of provisions for the sustenance of the tourists in the huts. The whole industry had become organised, and put on a financial basis. When the railway from Caernarfon to Llanberis was opened in 1869 visitors were greeted at the station by ponies and guides. Meanwhile from Beddgelert it cost seven shillings for a guide to the top during the day, ten by night. A pony cost an extra five shillings.

The opening of a road down to the coast made Snowdon accessible for the first time.

This increasing activity helps to explain why there was not more resistance to the building of the railway. Moreover we have to remember that the mood of the time permitted the wholesale industrialisation of the mountains, including Snowdon. The whole of the flanks above Cwm Dyli were pitted by copper mining by the mid 18th century, and these mines struggled on under different ownership until 1916. The workers spent the week in the huts still visible at Glaslyn and below Llydaw, walking home over the mountain largely to Beddgelert and Llanberis at the weekend. The copper ore was to begin with taken over the mountain too, by sledge, as the only access at the time to coastal ports. By 1832 the road from Pen y Pass to Llanberis was built, and the material could travel down to Caernarfon by crossing Llydaw by boat. Llydaw itself was lowered by twelve feet, in 1853, to enable the construction of the

Ruins of copper-mining works still lie above Llyn Llydaw.

The causeway over Llyn Llydaw was constructed in the mid 19th century to facilitate the copper mining.

The railway was completed in 1896.

causeway. Snowdon was in effect radically transformed by
this industrialization in the 19th century. The trackway by
which the ore slid down to the lake was, perhaps, the first
primitive form of Snowdon railway.

Railways had in fact been in use in connection with the
great quarries of the area for some time by then. In the
sixteenth century, when quarrying started, the stone was
brought down by waggonways. Lord Penrhyn built a track
in 1800 to connect his quarry with his port. The railway at
Nantlle of the 1920's was the first to carry passengers, and
the Ffestiniog quarry railway was designed from the start
for public transport. All these quarry railways had operated
by a combination of horse-power and gravity, until the
coming of steam in the 1860's made full mechanisation
possible. It was perhaps more in competition with what
became the Welsh Highland Railway, running from Dinas

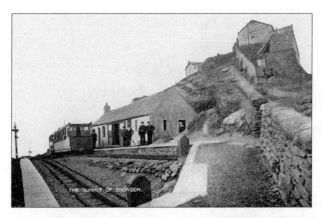

The first 'station' added to the sense of development of the summit.

near Caernarfon to Beddgelert, that the idea of initiating a line from Llanberis to the summit arose. A passenger service started to run from Dinas junction to Llyn Cwellyn in 1877, and on to the Snowdon Ranger in 1878, penetrating to Rhyd-ddu by 1881, and this was viewed by the people of Llanberis as a threat to their role as the tourist base for Snowdon.

The fact that the mountain railway did not come into existence earlier was due to the attitude of the landowner, George Assheton-Smith, owner of the Vaynol estate. When a bill was put before Parliament in 1871 to form a company to construct the railway it was opposed by Assheton-Smith on the grounds that it would spoil the scenery. The Assheton-Smith family had acquired an enclosure Act in 1806 which gave them ownership of a vast tract of country around Llanberis. It was not until the 1890's, by which time the station at Rhyd-ddu had been renamed 'Snowdon Station', that the threat to Llanberis's monopoly on

The summit 'station'.

Snowdon visiting convinced Assheton-Smith to change his mind, and 'The Snowdon Mountain Tramroad and Hotels Co Ltd' was formed. The new company acquired the required land from the Vaynol estate, a deal which included the lease of the Victoria Hotel.

The railway company had the difficult job of contending with those who already had interests there, and it was not until 1898 that they gained control of the whole summit, and built their own station building. There was still a residue of resistance to the whole thing. The intrusion of steam locomotion was a factor, and it was "greatly to be desired", says the 'Thorough Guide' of 1895, that "the intention to adopt electricity as the chief motive power will very soon be carried out."

...one cannot help expressing some sympathy for those so-called sentimentalists who look upon an engine puffing its way up the king of our mountains as a profanation of nature, however great a public benefit may accrue.

One clear dissenter, we are told, was the admirable Canon Rawnsley, who is much more famous for the good work he did in preserving the Lake District and for his part in founding the National Trust. Rawnsley had campaigned effectively to prevent slate railways operating from quarries above Buttermere, and he was afraid that the Snowdon example would lead to other such enterprises throughout Britain. On the whole, though, the reaction seems to have been acceptance of the inevitability of progress, in an age increasingly geared to the pleasures of the majority. Carr and Lister, who adopt a nostalgic tone in their book *The Mountains of Snowdonia* of 1925, admit reluctantly that "We are at the present day no more than on the threshold of the utilitarian age" and that 'the greatest good of the greatest number' may yet demand the sacrifice of much that we now hold dear. As regards the mountain railway:

> However much the lover of wild nature may regret its presence it serves two useful purposes. It gives pleasure and a small taste of the joy of the mountains to those who could not otherwise ascend the peak, and it conveys to the summit neatly packed in box-like coaches, the thousands whose one desire is to set foot on "the highest top."

With the successful acquisition of all the necessary land by the Tramway Company, and Assheton-Smith's acquiescence, any further legislation was avoided. The first sod was cut by him and his daughter Enid in December 1894. It is amazing that a few months later the bulk of the track was completed, and in less than two years the business was operating.

The method adopted for the eventual haulage was the 'Abt' system, called after Dr Abt, a Swiss engineer, which is conveniently classified as rack-and-pinion, and depends on interlocking cogs, on the train and the track.

It took 150 men to prepare the first two and a half miles of track by the end of March, 1895. The hardest part was the first: bridging the gorge across the river Hwch near to the base. Once the viaduct was built material could be brought up to the workpoint by train. The first engine had been delivered from Switzerland (where 'The Swiss Locomotive Manufactury' at Winterthur built the locomotives) in July, 1895. The first train actually reached the top on 9th January, 1896. A number of preliminary trials were then carried out, from January '96, and the formal opening took place on 6th April.It was however too late for it to be the first mountain railway in Britain, since the Snaefell railway on the Isle of Man had opened in August 1895.

It was Easter Monday. It was a notable occasion for the wrong sort of reason: about the only serious accident in the Railway's history took place. Although it was April, the conditions were bad: ice had formed under the rails, and when this thawed in the morning sun the track itself became uneven. For one reason or another the engine at the head of the downward journey came off the track, at the steepest part of the incline, and fell into Cwm Glas below. The driver and fireman succeeded in jumping clear, but one passenger was hurt when he tried to copy them, and sustained bad injuries, which later killed him through loss of blood. The toll could have been a great deal worse, were it not for the success of part of the system. The manager of the company who was travelling in the first coach behind the engine was able to apply the brakes with which the coaches are fitted, as the engine is not, as part of the system, attached to the train – pushing it on the way up, going ahead to check it on the way down. However the sequence of events continued to go wrong, making one feel that this could have been enough to put everyone off the whole idea. The loose engine brought down the cables carrying a telegraph system to the summit, where this effect apparently rang a bell, which was the signal for the train waiting there to leave. The mountain was in thick mist now, and so the next train ran into the carriages which had been stopped. Fortunately the positioning was such as to shuttle the whole lot into the loop of line where the trains now pass each other, at Clogwyn station. All the passengers then walked safely down to Llanberis.

The railway, not surprisingly, closed for a time, on the same occasion as it had opened. An inquiry recommended lighter loads to give slower speeds, and with modification of the rack system it reopened a year later. A 'gripper rail' was added which holds the engine onto the rail. With little interruption during the Fist World War and only some restriction during the Second it has gone on ever since. It has continued to use mainly steam engines (of which there are seven) but from 1986 two diesel engines have operated, now increased to four.

Rather more controversial than the railway over the years has been its 'station', the inevitable development from the 'hotel' which the huts had named themselves. Jenkins in fact recognizes two hotels, one alongside the railway platform and another perched high above it just below the summit. "It is regrettable," says a local guidebook of 1933, "that the views from the summit cairn are partially blotted out by buildings erected for the entertainment of tourists."

That was shortly before the erection of the construction which has most recently been demolished. Sir Clough Williams-Ellis was commissioned to build what was presumably intended to be the definitive summit hotel during the 1930's, his version being erected in 1934. It was hampered by the constraints of the site, flattened to lie inconspicuously below the summit. Clough himself, aware of its failure architecturally, complained that he was constrained by too many restrictions – implying, I think, the demands of bureaucratic requirements, as well as topography. The fact is the building was uncompromisingly practical and mundane in its character, a sort of prototype air-raid shelter, a concrete box with a flat roof, only the rather mean metal windows hinting at a contemporary style. Perhaps uniquely among Clough's countless buildings it showed no inclination to please. There was simply no joy about it.

Hafod Eryri

To the Present Day

The rise of rock-climbing as an independent pastime (succeeding mountaineering, or mountain climbing for another purpose) came at a time by which the summit itself had been thoroughly taken over by non-specialist visitors, in the early years of the twentieth century – and so, ironically, it hardly affects our story directly at all. Much that went on then around the mountain did not impinge on the top of it. In the early days however the skilled rock-climber would still pay lip-service to the idea of the purpose being to reach the peak. Geoffrey Winthrop Young, writing of the early twentieth century in *Snowdon Biography*, says that at that time "mountain climbing still meant going up mountains" and "rocks and cliffs were only incidents on the way." But the business quickly became more specialist. The difficulty which non-climbing walkers may find in sympathising with the recondite enthusiasm for gulleys and chimneys which impelled these fanatics is reminiscent of that of trying to appreciate the obsession with moss campion or mountain sorrel which drove the earlier explorers. The new generation egging each other on during the golden years before the Great War felt passionate about the rock, but no longer thought so much about the mountain.

Not that they were insensitive. It is clear that from the start (which may be dated as the foundation of the

Penygwryd

The Pen y Pass Group

Climbers' Club, Penygwryd based, in 1898) they were exceptional people, driven by a love of adventure and wild places, but at the same time scholarly and literary. When Winthrop Young himself led the move from the Penygwryd Hotel to the Pen y Pass he took with him a young crowd who would distinguish themselves in many impressive ways – people like Julian Huxley and Robert Graves. As he himself puts it:

> It has no importance for our climbing record, but it says something for the caliber of the men first attracted by the romance of the hills, and of pioneer climbing, that of those who came on Pen y Pass parties, as I look through the list of names, three

earned the Order of Merit, four had the Nobel Prize, five became Cabinet ministers, seven were made peers and one a life peer, fifteen were knighted, and of course an indefinite number became honorary doctors.

Like so much in British social history this period of self-discovery centred on Snowdon was cut short by the First World War; and when it tried to rediscover itself afterwards it was with a new attitude by a new class and with a different sort of clubbishness. This mass of activity around its flanks, particularly the long tradition (started, as we saw, by Bingley at the end of the 18th century) of climbing Clogwyn Du'r Arddu, continues, though developed rock-climbing has moved even further from Snowdon and its summit. Although the Pen y Pass Hotel has for a long time now been a Youth Hostel, the Penygwryd maintains its long association with the mountain, boosted by the association with Everest given it in the 1950's, when it was chosen as the base for training by the eventually victorious team led by Sir John Hunt.

Up on the top, away from much of this, Snowdon had in the meantime fallen piecemeal into public ownership. With the death of the last baronet a vast stretch of the Faenol estate, extending to the summit of Snowdon, was handed over to the nation, and thus became administered by the Welsh Office, now the Welsh Assembly, through the agency of the Snowdonia National Park Authority. The other part of the summit remained in the ownership of the farm of Hafod y Llan, in Nant Gwynant, until the owner of that farm decided to sell, resulting in the campaign of 1998

Construction work on Hafod Eryri.

to 'save Snowdon' for the nation, meaning effectively to raise funds to give Snowdon to the National Trust.

Perhaps it was the effect of the summit's being nationally owned and run by the National Park Authority that led to the development of an overall plan for the summit complex. In 2006 Clough's café was pulled down. It had become something of an embarrassment, in legend at least being referred to by the Prince of Wales as the highest slum in Wales. The Park Authority had started a public appeal for funds to rebuild it in 2001, and by 2006 a scheme for the replacement had emerged. Work started, first on the demolition, in March 2007. Hampered (as are all such schemes) by unexpected delays and rapidly expanding cost, the project finally got finished by the

A complex of plain concrete buildings had developed below the summit.

Construction of Hafod Eryri.

summer of 2009, when it was officially opened (on 12th June) by the First Minister of the Welsh Assembly.

Various firms were involved in its construction. The architects chosen were Furneaux Stewart, of London, who had worked on the Eden Project in Cornwall and the Welsh National Botanical Gardens. Ray Hole, architects, also of London were the architectural designers, and it was they who eventually won the Welsh Arts Council's Gold Medal for the result. The builders were an engineering firm called Carillion, based in Wolverhampton. In spite of its location at the heart of Wales, there is much about the building which is not Welsh. It is true, for instance, that the granite which forms the roof was imported from Portugal. Some of the stone making up the walls (in fact two-thirds of the whole materials) is indeed local, from Blaenau Ffestiniog. But the builders were under pressure to conform to a rigid timetable, and apparently the Portuguese supplier was better able to guarantee delivery than the local ones. The interior walls are lined with Welsh oak. At the time there was also much debate about whether the massive structure (in the end costing more than £8m) should have been built at all. It was felt by some that although some visitor facilities were necessary they could have been provided lower down, instead of actually on the summit. Any idea of keeping the summit natural and wild was however, by then, some two hundred years too late.

Hafod Eryri is the name which was chosen for the new building by the National Park Authority after a challenge on Radio Cymru produced 422 suggestions from a worldwide public. The Authority's committee finally voted from a shortlist of three, the others being Copa, the Welsh for summit or top, and Pen yr Wyddfa, the head of the tumulus. Hafod Eryri, the most suggestive, refers to the old habit of transhumance, by which an agricultural community would migrate into the uplands in the summer and live in its 'hafod', or summer dwelling.

Carillion decided that the structure should be fully investigated at ground level, and built the frame of it in a warehouse near Shotton on Deeside before dismantling it and transporting it in sections to Snowdon. It was considered too dangerous to carry the parts up by helicopter, and in the end everything went by train, much of the finishing taking place on site. Hafod Eryri is a self-consciously modern building, conforming to the current requirements of ecology. Rain is collected for waste uses; thermal insulation keeps the heat in. But it is not self-sufficient in energy, since it was considered to be too windy here for wind-power to be used, and too vulnerable to vandalism to have solar panels. It is powered by a generator, and drinking water has to be brought up on the train.

The execution of the concept behind it is masterly. It lies almost prone on the butt of the hillside, its grey flanks proclaiming, with quite remarkable forbearance, a positive, not a negative, reticence. This silent refusal to attempt any sort of statement, in a context where statements are redundant – having already, consummately, been made – is perhaps the hardest thing to achieve in architecture. Nothing you could think of could complement the implicit grandeur of the mountain.

All the greater is the shock of coming in from the mist and its total greyness and entering the world of automatic doors and a multilingual queue.

Hafod Eryri today.

Hafod Eryri's long battery of windows supports its essential nature: it is a viewpoint for a vision, a vision of extreme elevation, the end point of some sort of pilgrimage. Outside the eager crowd converges, as they always have done, ready for their turn to mount the summit cairn. Meanwhile at almost any time of the year a few thousand people are puffing and sweating up the mountain, with their dogs and children, their cameras and mobile phones; and the air of excitement at the whole idea is itself now a part of the spell of the place, making memorable the experience of being there.

The opening ceremony in June 2009.

The new summit station

Bibliography

Bennett, M. : *Geology of Snowdonia*, The Crowood Press, Marlborough. 2007

Bingley, Rev. W. : *North Wales*, Denbighshire County Council

Borrow, George : *Wild Wales*, Oxford University Press, 1946

Carr, H. R. C. and Lister, G. A. : *The Mountains of Snowdonia*, Bodley Head, London, 1925

Giraldus Cambrensis : *The Itinerary through Wales*, Everyman, 1935

Howell, M. F. : *Regional Guide to Wales* (Geological Survey).

Jenkins, D. E. : *Bedd Gelert*, Porthmadog, 1899. Facsimile Edition 1999, Friends of St Mary's Church, Beddgelert

Jones, D. : *The Botanists and Mountain Guides of Snowdonia*, Gwasg Carreg Gwalch, 1996

Jones, R. : *Yr Wyddfa – The Complete Guide to Snowdon*, Gwasg Carreg Gwalch, 1992

Kew, H. W. and Powell, H. E. : *Thomas Johnson, Botanist and Royalist*, Green & Co., London, 1932

Newell, R. H. : *Letters on the Scenery of Wales*, London, 1821; reprinted in facsimile, Bibliolife

North, F. J. (ed.) et.al. : *Snowdonia*, Collins, London, 1949

Noyce, E. (ed.) et.al. : *Snowdon Biography*, Dent, London, 1957

Watts-Dunton, T. : *Aylwin*, Oxford University Press, 1921

Wordsworth, W. ed. Ernest de Selincourt : *The Prelude*, Oxford University Press, 1926

Guide books

'Thorough Guide' series: *North Wales* M. J. B. Baddeley and C. S. Ward, London 1895

Gossiping Guide to Wales, London, 1898

Ward Lock & Co. *Llandudno and North Wales*, London, 1934

Other books by the same author

Visit our website for further information:
www.carreg-gwalch.com

Orders can be placed on our
On-line Shop

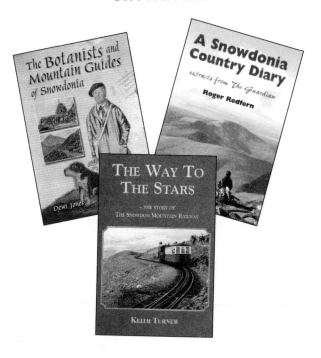